S0-ABB-659

THE ENLIGHTENMENT

History SparkNotes

Copyright © 2005 by Spark Educational Publishing

All rights reserved. No part of this book may be used or reproduced in any manner whatsoever without the written permission of the Publisher.

SPARKNOTES is a registered trademark of SparkNotes LLC

Spark Educational Publishing
A Division of Barnes & Noble Publishing
120 Fifth Avenue
New York, NY 10011
www.sparknotes.com

ISBN 1-4114-0429-7

Please submit all comments and questions or report errors to *www.sparknotes.com/errors*.

Printed and bound in the United States

CONTENTS

OVERVIEW

The Enlightenment was a sprawling intellectual, philosophical, cultural, and social movement that spread through England, France, Germany, and other parts of Europe during the 1700s. Enabled by the Scientific Revolution, which had begun as early as 1500, the Enlightenment represented about as big of a departure as possible from the Middle Ages—the period in European history lasting from roughly the fifth century to the fifteenth.

The millennium of the Middle Ages had been marked by unwavering religious devotion and unfathomable cruelty. Rarely before or after did the Church have as much power as it did during those thousand years. With the Holy Roman Empire as a foundation, missions such as the Crusades and Inquisition were conducted in part to find and persecute heretics, often with torture and death. Although standard at the time, such harsh injustices would eventually offend and scare Europeans into change. Science, though encouraged in the late Middle Ages as a form of piety and appreciation of God's creation, was frequently regarded as heresy, and those who tried to explain miracles and other matters of faith faced harsh punishment. Society was highly hierarchical, with serfdom a widespread practice. There were no mandates regarding personal liberties or rights, and many Europeans feared religion—either at the hands of an unmerciful God or at the hands of the sometimes brutal Church itself.

The Scientific Revolution and the Enlightenment, however, opened a path for independent thought, and the fields of mathematics, astronomy, physics, politics, economics, philosophy, and medicine were drastically updated and expanded. The amount of new knowledge that emerged was staggering. Just as important was the enthusiasm with which people approached the Enlightenment: intellectual salons popped up in France, philosophical discussions were held, and the increasingly literate population read books and passed them around feverishly. The Enlightenment and all of the new knowledge thus permeated nearly every facet of civilized life. Not everyone participated, as many uneducated, rural citizens were unable to share in the Enlightenment during its course. But even their time would come, as the Enlightenment also prompted the beginning of the Industrial Revolution, which provided rural dwellers with jobs and new cities in which to live.

Whether considered from an intellectual, political, or social standpoint, the advancements of the Enlightenment transformed the Western world into an intelligent and self-aware civilization. Moreover, it directly inspired the creation of the world's first great democracy, the United States of America. The new freedoms and ideas sometimes led to abuses—in particular, the descent of the French Revolution from a positive, productive coup into tyranny and bedlam. In response to the violence of the French Revolution, some Europeans began to blame the Enlightenment's attacks on tradition and breakdown of norms for inducing the anarchy.

Indeed, it took time for people to overcome this opinion and appreciate the Enlightenment's beneficial effect on their daily lives. But concrete, productive changes did, in fact, appear, under guises as varied as the ideas that inspired them. The effects of Enlightenment thought soon permeated both European and American life, from improved women's rights to more efficient steam engines, from fairer judicial systems to increased educational opportunities, from revolutionary economic theories to a rich array of literature and music.

These ideas, works, and principles of the Enlightenment would continue to affect Europe and the rest of the Western world for decades and even centuries to come. Nearly every theory or fact that is held in modern science has a foundation in the Enlightenment; in fact, many remain just as they were established. Yet it is not simply the knowledge attained during the Enlightenment that makes the era so pivotal—it's also the era's groundbreaking and tenacious new approaches to investigation, reasoning, and problem solving that make it so important. Never before had people been so vocal about making a difference in the world; although some may have been persecuted for their new ideas, it nevertheless became indisputable that thought had the power to incite real change. Just like calculus or free trade, the very concept of freedom of expression had to come from somewhere, and it too had firm roots in the Enlightenment.

SUMMARY OF EVENTS

CAUSES

On the surface, the most apparent cause of the Enlightenment was the **Thirty Years' War**. This horribly destructive war, which lasted from 1618 to 1648, compelled German writers to pen harsh criticisms regarding the ideas of nationalism and warfare. These authors, such as **Hugo Grotius** and **John Comenius**, were some of the first Enlightenment minds to go against tradition and propose better solutions.

At the same time, European thinkers' interest in the tangible world developed into **scientific study**, while greater **exploration** of the world exposed Europe to other cultures and philosophies. Finally, centuries of mistreatment at the hands of monarchies and the church brought average citizens in Europe to a breaking point, and the most intelligent and vocal finally decided to speak out.

PRE-ENLIGHTENMENT DISCOVERIES

The Enlightenment developed through a snowball effect: small advances triggered larger ones, and before Europe and the world knew it, almost two centuries of philosophizing and innovation had ensued. These studies generally began in the fields of earth science and astronomy, as notables such as **Johannes Kepler** and **Galileo Galilei** took the old, beloved "truths" of Aristotle and disproved them. Thinkers such as **René Descartes** and **Francis Bacon** revised the scientific method, setting the stage for **Isaac Newton** and his landmark discoveries in physics.

From these discoveries emerged a system for observing the world and making testable **hypotheses** based on those observations. At the same time, however, scientists faced ever-increasing scorn and skepticism from people in the religious community, who felt threatened by science and its attempts to explain matters of faith. Nevertheless, the progressive, rebellious spirit of these scientists would inspire a century's worth of thinkers.

THE ENLIGHTENMENT IN ENGLAND

The first major Enlightenment figure in England was **Thomas Hobbes**, who caused great controversy with the release of his provocative treatise *Leviathan* (1651). Taking a sociological perspective, Hobbes felt that by nature, people were self-serving and preoccupied with the gathering of a limited number of resources. To keep balance, Hobbes continued, it was essential to have a single intimidat-ing ruler. A half century later, **John Locke** came into the picture, promoting the opposite type of government—a representative gov-ernment—in his *Two Treatises of Government* (1690).

Although Hobbes would be more influential among his contem-poraries, it was clear that Locke's message was closer to the English people's hearts and minds. Just before the turn of the century, in 1688, English Protestants helped overthrow the Catholic king **James II** and installed the Protestant monarchs **William and Mary**. In the aftermath of this **Glorious Revolution**, the English government ratified a new Bill of Rights that granted more personal freedoms.

THE ENLIGHTENMENT IN FRANCE

Many of the major French Enlightenment thinkers, or **philosophes**, were born in the years after the Glorious Revolution, so France's Enlightenment came a bit later, in the mid-1700s. The philosophes, though varying in style and area of particular concern, generally emphasized the power of reason and sought to discover the natural laws governing human society. The **Baron de Montesquieu** tackled politics by elaborating upon Locke's work, solidifying concepts such as the **separation of power** by means of divisions in government. **Voltaire** took a more caustic approach, choosing to incite social and political change by means of satire and criticism. Although Vol-taire's satires arguably sparked little in the way of concrete change, Voltaire nevertheless was adept at exposing injustices and appealed to a wide range of readers. His short novel *Candide* is regarded as one of the seminal works in history.

Denis Diderot, unlike Montesquieu and Voltaire, had no revolu-tionary aspirations; he was interested merely in collecting as much knowledge as possible for his mammoth *Encyclopédie*. The *Ency-clopédie*, which ultimately weighed in at thirty-five volumes, would go on to spread Enlightenment knowledge to other countries around the world.

ROMANTICISM

In reaction to the rather empirical philosophies of Voltaire and others, **Jean-Jacques Rousseau** wrote *The Social Contract* (1762), a work championing a form of government based on small, direct democracy that directly reflects the will of the population. Later, at the end of his career, he would write *Confessions,* a deeply personal reflection on his life. The unprecedented intimate perspective that Rousseau provided

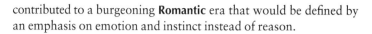

contributed to a burgeoning **Romantic** era that would be defined by an emphasis on emotion and instinct instead of reason.

SKEPTICISM

Another undercurrent that threatened the prevailing principles of the Enlightenment was **skepticism**. Skeptics questioned whether human society could really be perfected through the use of reason and denied the ability of rational thought to reveal universal truths. Their philosophies revolved around the idea that the perceived world is relative to the beholder and, as such, no one can be sure whether any truths actually exist.

Immanuel Kant, working in Germany during the late eighteenth century, took skepticism to its greatest lengths, arguing that man could truly know neither observed objects nor metaphysical concepts; rather, the experience of such things depends upon the psyche of the observer, thus rendering universal truths impossible. The theories of Kant, along with those of other skeptics such as **David Hume**, were influential enough to change the nature of European thought and effectively end the Enlightenment.

THE END OF THE ENLIGHTENMENT

Ultimately, the Enlightenment fell victim to competing ideas from several sources. Romanticism was more appealing to less-educated common folk and pulled them away from the empirical, scientific ideas of earlier Enlightenment philosophers. Similarly, the theories of skepticism came into direct conflict with the reason-based assertions of the Enlightenment and gained a following of their own.

What ultimately and abruptly killed the Enlightenment, however, was the **French Revolution**. Begun with the best intentions by French citizens inspired by Enlightenment thought, the revolution attempted to implement orderly representative assemblies but quickly degraded into chaos and violence. Many people cited the Enlightenment-induced breakdown of norms as the root cause of the instability and saw the violence as proof that the masses could not be trusted to govern themselves. Nonetheless, the discoveries and theories of the Enlightenment philosophers continued to influence Western society for centuries.

KEY PEOPLE & TERMS

PEOPLE

JOHANN SEBASTIAN BACH (1685–1750)
An enormously influential German composer who rose to prominence in the early 1700s. Best known by his contemporaries as an organist, Bach also wrote an enormous body of both sacred and secular music that synthesized a variety of styles and in turn influenced countless later composers.

FRANCIS BACON (1561–1626)
An English philosopher and statesman who developed the **inductive method** or **Baconian method** of scientific investigation, which stresses observation and reasoning as a means for coming to general conclusions. Bacon's work influenced his later contemporary **René Descartes**.

CESARE BECCARIA (1738–1794)
An Italian politician who ventured into philosophy to protest the horrible injustices that he observed in various European judicial systems. Beccaria's book *On Crimes and Punishments* (1764) exposed these practices and led to the abolition of many.

JOHN COMENIUS (1592–1670)
A Czech educational and social reformer who, in response to the **Thirty Years' War**, made the bold move of challenging the necessity of war in the first place. Comenius stressed tolerance and education as alternatives for war, which were revolutionary concepts at the time.

RENÉ DESCARTES (1596–1650)
A French philosopher and scientist who revolutionized algebra and geometry and made the famous philosophical statement "I think, therefore I am." Descartes developed a **deductive** approach to philosophy using math and logic that still remains a standard for problem solving.

DENIS DIDEROT (1713–1784)
A French scholar who was the primary editor of the *Encyclopédie*, a massive thirty-five-volume compilation of human knowledge in the arts and sciences, along with commentary from a number of

Enlightenment thinkers. The *Encyclopédie* became a prominent symbol of the Enlightenment and helped spread the movement throughout Europe.

BENJAMIN FRANKLIN (1706–1790)
American thinker, diplomat, and inventor who traveled frequently between the American colonies and Europe during the Enlightenment and facilitated an exchange of ideas between them. Franklin exerted profound influence on the formation of the new government of the United States, with a hand in both the **Declaration of Independence** and the **U.S. Constitution**.

JOHANN WOLFGANG VON GOETHE (1749–1832)
A German author who wrote near the end of the **Aufklärung**, the German Enlightenment. Goethe's morose *The Sorrows of Young Werther* (1774) helped fuel the *Sturm und Drang* movement, and his two-part *Faust* (1808, 1832) is seen as one of the landmarks of Western literature.

OLYMPE DE GOUGES (1748–1793)
A French feminist and reformer in the waning years of the Enlightenment who articulated the rights of women with her *Declaration of the Rights of Woman and the Female Citizen* (1791).

HUGO GROTIUS (1583–1645)
A Dutch scholar who, like Czech **John Comenius**, lived during the **Thirty Years' War** and felt compelled to write in response to it. The result, a treatise on war and international relations titled *On the Law of War and Peace* (1625), eventually became accepted as the basis for the rules of modern warfare.

GEORGE FRIDERIC HANDEL (1685–1759)
A German-English composer of the late Baroque period whose *Messiah* remains one of the best-known pieces of music in the world. Handel was an active court composer, receiving commissions from such notables as King George I of England, for whom his *Water Music* suite was written and performed.

THOMAS HOBBES (1588–1679)
A philosopher and political theorist whose 1651 treatise *Leviathan* effectively kicked off the English Enlightenment. The controversial *Leviathan* detailed Hobbes's theory that all humans are inherently self-driven and evil and that the best form of government is thus a single, all-powerful monarch to keep everything in order.

DAVID HUME (1711–1776)

A Scottish philosopher and one of the most prominent figures in the field of **skepticism** during the Enlightenment. Hume took religion to task, asking why a perfect God would ever create an imperfect world, and even suggested that our own senses are fallible, bringing all observations and truths into question. Hume's skepticism proved very influential to others, such as **Immanuel Kant**, and was instrumental in the shift away from rationalist thought that ended the Enlightenment.

THOMAS JEFFERSON (1743–1826)

American thinker and politician who penned the **Declaration of Independence** (1776), which was inspired directly by Enlightenment thought.

IMMANUEL KANT (1724–1804)

A German skeptic philosopher who built on **David Hume**'s theories and brought the school of thought to an even higher level. Kant theorized that all humans are born with innate "experiences" that then reflect onto the world, giving them a perspective. Thus, since no one actually knows what other people see, the idea of "reasoning" is not valid. Kant's philosophies applied the brakes to the Enlightenment, effectively denouncing reason as an invalid approach to thought.

GOTTFRIED WILHELM LEIBNIZ (1646–1716)

Generally considered the founder of the **Aufklärung**, or German Enlightenment, who injected a bit of spirituality into the Enlightenment with writings regarding God and his perfect, harmonious world. Also a scientist who shared credit for the discovery of **calculus**, Leibniz hated the idea of relying on empirical evidence in the world. Instead, he developed a theory that the universe consists of metaphysical building blocks he called **monads**.

JOHN LOCKE (1632–1704)

An English political theorist who focused on the structure of governments. Locke believed that men are all rational and capable people but must compromise some of their beliefs in the interest of forming a government for the people. In his famous *Two Treatises of Government* (1690), he championed the idea of a representative government that would best serve all constituents.

BARON DE MONTESQUIEU (1689–1755)

The foremost French political thinker of the Enlightenment, whose most influential book, *The Spirit of Laws,* expanded **John Locke**'s political study and incorporated the ideas of a division of state and separation of powers. Montesquieu's work also ventured into sociology: he spent a considerable amount of time researching various cultures and their climates, ultimately deducing that climate is a major factor in determining the type of government a given country should have.

WOLFGANG AMADEUS MOZART (1756–1791)

A genius Austrian composer who began his career as a child prodigy and authored some of the most renowned operas and symphonies in history. Mozart's music has never been surpassed in its blend of technique and emotional breadth, and his musical genius places him in a category with a select few other composers.

SIR ISAAC NEWTON (1642–1727)

An English scholar and mathematician regarded as the father of physical science. Newton's discoveries anchored the Scientific Revolution and set the stage for everything that followed in mathematics and physics. He shared credit for the creation of **calculus**, and his *Philosophiae Naturalis Principia Mathematica* introduced the world to **gravity** and fundamental **laws of motion**.

THOMAS PAINE (1737–1809)

English-American political writer whose pamphlet *Common Sense* (1776) argued that the British colonies in America should rebel against the Crown. Paine's work had profound influence on public sentiment during the **American Revolution**, which had begun just months earlier.

FRANÇOIS QUESNAY (1694–1774)

A French economist whose *Tableau Économique* (1758) argued against government intervention in the economy and inspired Scottish economist **Adam Smith**'s seminal *Wealth of Nations* (1776).

JEAN-JACQUES ROUSSEAU (1712–1778)

An eclectic Swiss-French thinker who brought his own approach to the Enlightenment, believing that man was at his best when unshackled by the conventions of society. Rousseau's epic *The Social Contract* (1762) conceived of a system of direct democracy in which all citizens contribute to an overarching "general will" that serves everyone at once. Later in his life, Rousseau released *Confessions* (1789), which brought a previously unheard-of degree of personal disclosure to the genre of autobiography. The frank personal revelations and emotional discussions were a major cause for the shift toward Romanticism.

ADAM SMITH (1723–1790)

An influential Scottish economist who objected to the stifling **mercantilist** systems that were in place during the late eighteenth century. In response, Smith wrote the seminal *Wealth of Nations* (1776), a dissertation criticizing mercantilism and describing the many merits of a free trade system.

BARUCH SPINOZA (1632–1677)

A Dutch-Jewish lens grinder who questioned tenets of Judaism and Christianity, which helped undermine religious authority in Europe. Although Spinoza personally believed in God, he rejected the concept of miracles, the religious supernatural, and the idea that the Bible was divinely inspired. Rather, he believed that ethics determined by rational thought were more important as a guide to conduct than was religion.

VOLTAIRE (1694–1778)

A French writer and the primary satirist of the Enlightenment, who criticized religion and leading philosophies of the time. Voltaire's numerous plays and essays frequently advocated freedom from the ploys of religion, while *Candide* (1759), the most notable of his works, conveyed his criticisms of optimism and superstition into a neat package.

TERMS

AUFKLÄRUNG

Another name for the **German Enlightenment**.

DEISM

A system of faith to which many of the French **philosophes** and other Enlightenment thinkers subscribed. Deists believed in an all-powerful God but viewed him as a "cosmic watchmaker" who created the universe and set it in autonomous motion and then never again tampered with it. Deists also shunned organized religion, especially Church doctrines about eternal damnation and a "natural" hierarchy of existence.

ENLIGHTENED ABSOLUTISM

A trend in European governments during the later part of the Enlightenment, in which a number of **absolute monarchs** adopted

Enlightenment-inspired reforms yet retained a firm grip on power. **Frederick the Great** of Prussia, **Maria-Theresa** and **Joseph II** of Austria, **Charles III** of Spain, and **Catherine the Great** of Russia are often counted among these "enlightened despots."

FRENCH REVOLUTION

A revolution in France that overthrew the monarchy and is often cited as the end of the Enlightenment. The French Revolution began in 1789 when King **Louis XVI** convened the legislature in an attempt to solve France's monumental financial woes. Instead, the massive middle class revolted and set up its own government. Although this new government was effective for a few years, internal dissent grew and power switched hands repeatedly, until France plunged into the brutally violent Reign of Terror of 1793–1794. Critics saw this violence as a direct result of Enlightenment thought and as evidence that the masses were not fit to govern themselves.

GLORIOUS REVOLUTION

The name given to the bloodless coup d'état in England in 1688, which saw the Catholic monarch, King **James II**, removed from the throne and replaced by the Protestants **William and Mary**. The new monarchs not only changed the religious course of England and the idea of divine right but also allowed the additional personal liberties necessary for the Enlightenment to truly flourish.

INDIVIDUALISM

One of the cornerstones of the Enlightenment, a philosophy stressing the recognition of every person as a valuable individual with inalienable, inborn rights.

MERCANTILISM

The economic belief that a favorable balance of trade—that is, more exports than imports—would yield more gold and silver, and thus overall wealth and power, for a country. Governments tended to monitor and meddle with their mercantilist systems closely, which Scottish economist **Adam Smith** denounced as bad economic practice in his *Wealth of Nations.*

PHILOSOPHES

The general term for those academics and intellectuals who became the leading voices of the **French Enlightenment** during the eighteenth century. Notable philosophes included **Voltaire**, the **Baron de Montesquieu**, and **Denis Diderot**.

RATIONALISM
Arguably the foundation of the Enlightenment, the belief that, by using the power of reason, humans could arrive at truth and improve human life.

RELATIVISM
Another fundamental philosophy of the Enlightenment, which declared that different ideas, cultures, and beliefs had equal merit. Relativism developed in reaction to the age of exploration, which increased European exposure to a variety of peoples and cultures across the world.

ROMANTICISM
A movement that surfaced near the end of the Enlightenment that placed emphasis on innate emotions and instincts rather than reason, as well as on the virtues of existing in a natural state. Writers such as **Jean-Jacques Rousseau** and **Johann Wolfgang von Goethe** both contributed greatly to the development of Romanticism.

SALONS
Gathering places for wealthy, intellectually minded elites during the years during and prior to the Enlightenment. The salons typically held weekly meetings where upper-class citizens gathered to discuss the political and social theories of the day.

SCIENTIFIC REVOLUTION
A gradual development of thought and approaches to the study of the universe that took place from approximately 1500 to 1700 and paved the way for the Enlightenment. Coming from humble beginnings with basic observations, the Scientific Revolution grew to a fever pitch when scientists such as **Galileo Galilei**, **René Descartes**, and **Johannes Kepler** entered the scene and essentially rewrote history, disproving Church doctrines, explaining religious "miracles," and setting the world straight on all sorts of scientific principles. The result was not only new human knowledge but also a new perspective on the acquisition of knowledge, such as the **scientific method**.

SEPARATION OF POWER
A political idea, developed by **John Locke** and the **Baron de Montesquieu**, that power in government should be divided into separate branches—typically legislative, judicial, and executive—in order to ensure that no one branch of a governing body can gain too much authority.

SKEPTICISM

A philosophical movement that emerged in response to **rationalism** and maintained that human perception is too relative to be considered credible. **David Hume** brought skepticism into the spotlight by suggesting that human perceptions cannot be trusted, and then **Immanuel Kant** elevated the field when he proposed that humans are born with innate "experiences" that give shape to their own, individual worlds.

SOCIAL CONTRACT

An idea in political philosophy, generally associated with **John Locke** and **Jean-Jacques Rousseau**, stating that a government and its subjects enter into an implicit contract when that government takes power. In exchange for ceding some freedoms to the government and its established laws, the subjects expect and demand mutual protection. The government's authority, meanwhile, lies only in the consent of the governed.

STURM UND DRANG

Literally meaning "storm and stress," the name given to an undercurrent of the **German Enlightenment** during which German youths expressed their angst by rebelling against the pleasant optimism of the time. Influenced partly by **Johann Wolfgang von Goethe**'s *The Sorrows of Young Werther*, participants in the *Sturm und Drang* movement harbored a depressed, more archaic idealism. Though it revealed a decided one-sidedness of the German Enlightenment, the movement did not sustain itself for very long.

THIRTY YEARS' WAR

A brutal, destructive conflict in Germany between 1618 and 1648. The Thirty Years' War began when Bohemian Protestants revolted out of a refusal to be ruled by a Catholic king. The battle would eventually spread throughout Germany and involve many other countries on both sides, resulting in the death of nearly a third of the German population and unfathomable destruction. Enlightenment thinkers such as **John Comenius** and **Hugo Grotius** reacted against the war with treatises about education, international relations, and the nature of war itself.

Summary & Analysis

The Roots of the Enlightenment

Events

1605	Kepler discovers first law of planetary motion
1609	Galileo develops his first telescope
1618	Thirty Years' War begins
1625	Grotius publishes *On the Law of War and Peace*
1633	Pope prosecutes Galileo for promoting sun-centered theory of the solar system
1648	Thirty Years' War ends
1687	Newton publishes *Philosophiae Naturalis Principia Mathematica*

Key People

Galileo Galilei Italian astronomer who supported the sun-centered Copernican model of the solar system, angering the Catholic Church

Johannes Kepler German astronomer who discovered laws of planetary motion

Francis Bacon English scholar who developed inductive method of reasoning

René Descartes French mathematician and philosopher who revolutionized algebra and geometry, developed deductive method

Isaac Newton English mathematician and physicist who formulated fundamental laws of gravity and motion

Baruch Spinoza Dutch-Jewish thinker who questioned many tenets of Judaism and Christianity

John Comenius Czech reformer who questioned necessity for war

Hugo Grotius Dutch scholar who explored concepts in international relations and outlined laws of "fair" warfare

The Scientific Revolution

The Enlightenment was the product of a vast set of cultural and intellectual changes in Europe during the 1500s and 1600s—changes that in turn produced the social values that permitted the Enlightenment to sweep through Europe in the late 1600s and 1700s. One of the most important of these changes was the **Scientific Revolution** of the 1500s and 1600s. During the Scientific Revolution, European thinkers tore down the flawed set of "scientific" beliefs established by the ancients and maintained by the Church. To replace this flawed knowledge, scientists sought to discover and convey the true laws governing the phenomena they observed in nature.

Although it would take centuries to develop, the Scientific Revolution began near the end of the **Middle Ages,** when farmers began to notice, study, and record those environmental conditions that yielded the best harvests. In time, curiosity about the world spread, which led to further innovation. Even the Church initially encouraged such investigations, out of the belief that studying the world was a form of piety and constituted an admiration of God's work.

GALILEO AND KEPLER

The Church's benevolent stance toward science changed abruptly when astronomers such as **Galileo Galilei** (1564–1642) and **Johannes Kepler** (1571–1630) started questioning the ancient teachings of Aristotle and other accepted "truths." Galileo's work in the fields of physics and inertia was groundbreaking, while Kepler's laws of planetary motion revealed, among other things, that the planets moved in elliptical orbits. Galileo especially encountered significant resistance from the Church for his support of the theories of Polish astronomer **Nicolaus Copernicus** (1473–1543), who had stated that the sun, not the earth, was the center of the solar system—not vice versa, as Church teaching had always maintained.

BACON AND DESCARTES

Though up against considerable Church opposition, science moved into the spotlight in the late 1500s and early 1600s. Galileo had long said that **observation** was a necessary element of the **scientific method**—a point that **Francis Bacon** (1561–1626) solidified with his inductive method. Sometimes known as the **Baconian method**, inductive science stresses observation and reasoning as the means for coming to general conclusions.

A later contemporary, **René Descartes** (1596–1650), picked up where Bacon left off. Descartes' talents ran the gamut from mathematics to philosophy and ultimately the combination of those schools. His work in combining algebra and geometry revolutionized both of those fields, and it was Descartes who came to the philosophical conclusion "I think, therefore I am"—asserting that, if nothing else, he was at least a thinking being. Descartes' **deductive** approach to philosophy, using math and logic, stressed a "clear and distinct foundation for thought" that still remains a standard for problem solving.

NEWTON

As it turned out, all of these developments of the Scientific Revolution were really just a primer for Englishman **Isaac Newton** (1642–1727), who swept in, built upon the work of his predecessors, and changed the face of science and mathematics. Newton began his career with mathematics work that would eventually evolve into the entire field of **calculus**. From there, he conducted experiments in physics and math that revealed a number of natural laws that had previously been credited to divine forces. Newton's seminal work, the ***Philosophiae Naturalis Principia Mathematica*** (1687), discussed the existence of a uniform force of **gravity** and established three **laws of motion**. Later in his career, Newton would release *Optics*, which detailed his groundbreaking work in that field as well.

THE LEGACY OF THE SCIENTIFIC REVOLUTION

During the Scientific Revolution, physics, philosophy, earth science, astronomy, and mathematics all experienced bold new innovation. Even more significant, the *methods* of scientific exploration were refined. The thinkers of the Scientific Revolution generated the concepts of inductive and deductive reasoning, as well as the general observe-hypothesize-experiment methodology known as the scientific method. Ultimately, these movements yielded the work of Newton, who is considered one of the most influential scientists of all time. His approach to the world encouraged observation and the realization not of causes but of effects. Just as important, Newton showed that scientific thought and methods could be applied to nonscientific topics—a development that paved the way for numerous later thinkers of the Enlightenment.

EXPLORATION AND IMPERIALISM

In addition to these scientific milestones, political and cultural change was taking place in Europe as the result of **exploration** and the extension of overseas **empires**, especially in the Americas. In addition to the brand-new discovery of America, European explorers also used new transportation technologies to explore already-known locales in Africa and Asia in greater depth than ever before.

As these explorers returned from across the world with stories of peoples and cultures never previously known, Europeans were introduced to drastically different lifestyles and beliefs. Some explorers brought foreign visitors to Europe, which introduced common people—who wouldn't otherwise be able to travel—to these foreign influences. The Orient especially mystified Europeans: its religions, familial relationships, and scientific discoveries astounded Westerners to such a degree that the emulation of Chinese culture briefly came into fashion. All in all, this worldlier perspective provided Enlightenment-era thinkers with the inspiration and impetus for change.

THE DECLINING INFLUENCE OF THE CHURCH

Yet another major change in the lives of Europeans prior to the Enlightenment was the weakening of adherence to traditional religious authority. The questioning of religion itself can largely be traced to the tensions created by the **Protestant Reformation**, which split the Catholic Church and opened new territory for theological debate. Additional seeds were planted by **Baruch Spinoza** (1632–1677), a Jewish lens grinder and philosopher from Amsterdam who developed a philosophy emphasizing ethical thought as the guide to conduct. Spinoza called into question the tenets of both Judaism and Christianity: he believed in God but denied that the Bible was divinely inspired and rejected the concept of miracles and the religious supernatural. He claimed that ethics determined by rational thought were more important as a guide to conduct than was religion.

As other seventeenth-century thinkers similarly questioned the authority of organized religion, it became much more common in European intellectual circles to put the concepts of religious belief to question. Although the Church's influence still remained strong, especially among the lower classes, the ideas of Spinoza combined with the new discoveries of the Scientific Revolution threatened the supremacy of Church doctrine considerably. Most devastating was the philosophical approach many scientists were taking, which often led to conclusions that God either did not exist or at least did not play much of a role in daily life.

Moreover, these advances in thought coincided with anti-church and government sentiment that was already growing among European commoners. The Catholic Church at the time was famously corrupt, and it often ruled using intimidation, fear, and false knowledge and was violently intolerant toward dissenters and heretics. Subsequently, when Enlightenment philosophers came along praising liberty and self-empowerment, they found willing ears.

THE THIRTY YEARS' WAR

Another major change in Europe prior to the Enlightenment was an increased questioning of the justness of **absolute monarchy**. For centuries, the common citizens of Europe had little or no role in their governments. During the seventeenth and eighteenth centuries, however, developments occurred that caused the authority of European **divine right**—the idea that monarchs were infallible because their titles were granted by God—to weaken. Perhaps the most

SUMMARY & ANALYSIS

immediate catalyst of the Enlightenment in this regard was the **Thirty Years' War**, which broke out in 1618 when Bohemian Protestants revolted against their incoming Catholic king. The ensuing battle between Protestants and Catholics spread into Germany, and over the course of the next thirty years, nearly a third of the German population was killed.

THE FIRST ENLIGHTENMENT THOUGHT

The atrocities that the German public endured over those three decades inspired leading European thinkers and writers to decry war as an institution. Czech reformer **John Comenius** (1592–1670) questioned the necessity of war, emphasizing the similarity of man by writing that "we are all citizens of one world, we are all of one blood." Meanwhile, Dutch thinker **Hugo Grotius** (1583–1645) wrote that the right of an individual to live and exist peacefully transcends any responsibility to a government's idea of national duty. Grotius's desire for humane treatment in wartime was expressed in his *On the Law of War and Peace* (1625), which proposed such wartime policies as the declaration of war, the honoring of treaties, and humane treatment of war prisoners.

Comenius's and Grotius's antiwar sentiments were the first developments of the Enlightenment in the sense that they went against tradition and took a humanistic approach to the atrocities in the world. Grotius was perhaps most significant for defining the God-given duties of man and then showing how war infringed upon them, thus "proving" that war is wrong. Comenius, for his part, went so far as to question the idea of nationalism and the obligation one has to give one's life for one's country.

INDIVIDUALISM, RELATIVISM, AND RATIONALISM

Ultimately, from this slew of scientific, cultural, social, and political developments in Europe during the sixteenth and seventeenth centuries emerged three fundamental ideas that encompassed everything the Enlightenment would stand for. First among these was **individualism**, which emphasized the importance of the individual and his inborn rights. The second, **relativism**, was the concept that different cultures, beliefs, ideas, and value systems had equal merit. Finally, **rationalism** was the conviction that with the power of reason, humans could arrive at truth and improve the world.

These three ideas reveal the fundamental concepts that would pervade the Enlightenment—man's ability to reason, to look past

SUMMARY & ANALYSIS

the traditions and conventions that had dominated Europe in the past, and to make decisions for himself. Moreover, these ideas represented the separation and autonomy of man's intellect from God—a development that opened the door to new discoveries and ideas and threatened the most powerful of Europe's long-standing institutions.

SUMMARY & ANALYSIS

THE ENGLISH ENLIGHTENMENT

EVENTS

1649	English Civil War overthrows Charles I, installs Cromwell
1651	Hobbes publishes *Leviathan*
1688	Glorious Revolution unseats James II, installs William and Mary
1689	English Bill of Rights drafted
1690	Locke publishes *Essay Concerning Human Understanding* and *Two Treatises of Government*

KEY PEOPLE

Thomas Hobbes Pessimistic English political philosopher; argued that man in his natural state is selfish and savage and therefore a single absolute ruler is the best form of government

John Locke Optimistic English political philosopher; argued for man's essentially good nature; advocated representative government as an ideal form

THE ENGLISH CIVIL WAR

Seventeenth-century England endured a pair of tense struggles for political power that had a profound impact on the philosophers of the **English Enlightenment**. The first power struggle came in 1649, when the **English Civil War** resulted in the execution of King **Charles I** and the establishment of a commonwealth under **Oliver Cromwell**. Although this republic endured for a decade, it also essentially devolved into dictatorship, and England ended up reverting to monarchy with the restoration of **Charles II** to the throne.

THE GLORIOUS REVOLUTION

The reestablished monarchy had clear limits placed on its absolute power, however, as was made clear in the bloodless **Glorious Revolution** of 1688, in which the English people overthrew a king they deemed unacceptable and basically chose their next rulers. The revolution occurred because Charles II's son, **James II**, was an overt Catholic, which did not sit well with the predominantly Protestant public. The English people rallied behind James II's Protestant daughter, **Mary**, and her husband, **William of Orange**, who led a nonviolent coup that dethroned James II and sent him to France. When William and Mary ascended the throne, they effectively ended the Catholic monarchy and the idea of divine right. In the years that followed, an English **Bill of Rights** was drafted, boosting parliamentary power and personal liberties. In this freer environment, science, the arts, and philosophy flourished.

HOBBES

The first major figure in the English Enlightenment was the political philosopher **Thomas Hobbes** (1588–1679), who began his career as a tutor but branched out to philosophy around the age of thirty. In 1640, fearing that some of his writings had angered England's parliament, Hobbes fled to Paris, where he penned a substantial body of his work. He is best known for the epic ***Leviathan*** (1651), a lengthy, groundbreaking work that explores human nature.

In *Leviathan*, Hobbes elaborates on the nature of man and justifies absolutist rule. He argues that human nature is inherently bad and that humans will remain in a constant a state of war, vying for power and material resources, unless awed by a single great power. However, Hobbes also claims that any group of men who ascend to positions of great power will be prone to abusing it, seeking more power than necessary for the stability of society. Thus, he reasons, a single absolute ruler is better than an oligarchy or democracy; because that ruler's wealth and power is largely equivalent to the wealth and power of the nation, he will seek to lead the nation on a stable and prosperous course. Hobbes claims that this sovereign's main duty is to provide protection to the citizens and that if he fails at that task, allegiance may be transferred to another.

An atheist, Hobbes long argued that religion is useful as a propaganda machine for the state, as it is the entity most capable of reminding the ignorant masses of their role and their duties. He was of the opinion that human life is by nature "solitary, poor, nasty, brutish and short" and was pessimistic about the prospects for progress in a world short on ethics. Fearing, justly, that *Leviathan* might offend certain groups—especially Anglicans and French Catholics—Hobbes figured himself safest at home and returned to London, where he lived out his years privately.

Commentators have praised Hobbes's work for its logic and clarity but have disagreed over precisely what he meant. For instance, the rules Hobbes sets forth as to precisely when a citizen may transfer allegiance to a new sovereign are unclear. Basically, only when a ruler kills or ceases to protect a subject may a subject oppose the ruler; at all other times, the subject must remain subservient. The greatest criticism of Hobbes focuses on his failure to describe how totally selfish men would be able to create and maintain the covenant of the state. Hobbes avoids the errors inherent in assuming that all human beings are inherently virtuous, but he is hard-pressed to explain how humans would behave in the manner he describes if they are inherently stupid. Hobbes represents the pessimistic side of the Enlightenment and sees progress as the result of the *suppression* of man's instincts rather than the granting of freedom to those instincts.

LOCKE

On the opposite side of the spectrum from the pessimistic Hobbes was **John Locke** (1632–1704), the other major English political philosopher of the seventeenth century. Locke received a prestigious education throughout his youth and remained involved in academics long after graduation. It was while dabbling in medicine with a mentor that he was introduced to political thought, which then captured his interest.

Locke's early writings focus on the religious intolerance and bickering that was blighting England at the time. Though important, these earlier works did not have nearly the influence or prominence of later works such as *Essay Concerning Human Understanding* (1690), in which Locke puts forth his optimistic idea that man's mind is a blank slate and that man can subsequently learn and improve through conscious effort. Locke followed with the work for which he is even better known, *Two Treatises of Government* (also 1690). This political work was massively influential, particularly the second treatise, and is still considered the foundation for modern political thought.

Not surprisingly, Locke's more optimistic work was more warmly received and more influential than Hobbes's in the long run. In particular, Locke's second treatise on government—which details Locke's belief that every man is inherently good but that the necessity of government requires that people compromise on some issues for the betterment of the whole—has endured. The work sets forth Locke's ideas for an ideal **representative government** and makes suggestions that would eventually be elaborated into ideas such as **separation of powers**—the system that the founding fathers of the United States used when writing the U.S. Constitution.

THE FRENCH ENLIGHTENMENT

EVENTS

1715	Louis XIV dies; Louis XV takes French throne
1748	Montesquieu publishes *The Spirit of Laws*
1751	Diderot publishes first volume of *Encyclopédie*
1759	Voltaire publishes *Candide*

KEY PEOPLE

Louis XIV "Sun King" whose late-1600s extravagance prompted disgruntled French elites to congregate in salons and exchange ideas

Louis XV Successor to Louis XIV; ineffective ruler who allowed France to slide into bankruptcy; ineptness greatly undermined authority of French monarchy

Baron de Montesquieu Philosopher whose *The Spirit of Laws* (1748) built on Locke's ideas about government

Voltaire Primary satirist of the French Enlightenment; best known for *Candide* (1759)

Denis Diderot Primary editor of the mammoth *Encyclopédie*, which attempted to aggregate all human knowledge into one work

SUMMARY & ANALYSIS

ORIGINS OF THE FRENCH ENLIGHTENMENT

Although the first major figures of the Enlightenment came from England, the movement truly exploded in France, which became a hotbed of political and intellectual thought in the 1700s. The roots of this **French Enlightenment** lay largely in resentment and discontent over the decadence of the French monarchy in the late 1600s. During the reign of the wildly extravagant "Sun King" **Louis XIV** (reigned 1643–1715), wealthy intellectual elites began to gather regularly in Parisian **salons** (often hosted by high-society women) and complain about the state of their country. The salons only grew in popularity when Louis XIV died and the far less competent **Louis XV** took over.

Gradually, complaints in the salons and coffee shops changed from idle whining into constructive political thought. Especially after the works of John Locke became widespread, participants at the salons began to discuss substantive political and social philosophies of the day. Before long, cutting-edge thought in a variety of disciplines worked its way into the salons, and the French Enlightenment was born.

THE PHILOSOPHES

By the early 1700s, coffee shops, salons, and other social groups were popping up all over Paris, encouraging intellectual discussion regarding the political and philosophical status of the country. Moreover, members of these groups increasingly clamored to read the latest work of leading philosophers. These nontraditional think-ers came to be known as the **philosophes**, a group that championed personal liberties and the work of Locke and Newton, denounced Christianity, and actively opposed the abusive governments found throughout Europe at the time. As varied as they were, the leading French philosophes generally came from similar schools of thought. They were predominantly writers, journalists, and teachers and were confident that human society could be improved through rational thought.

PHILOSOPHES AND THE CHURCH
A large part of the philosophes' attacks were focused on the Church and its traditions. In matters of faith, many of the prominent philos-ophes were **deists**—they believed in an all-powerful being but lik-ened him to a "cosmic watchmaker" who simply set the universe in autonomous motion and never again tampered with it. Moreover, they disdained organized religion and the Church's traditional idea of the "chain of being," which implied a natural hierarchy of existence—God first, then angels, monarchs, aristocrats, and so on.

The philosophes also raised objections against the decadent life-styles of leading Church representatives, as well as the Church's persistence in collecting exorbitant taxes and tithes from the com-moners to fund outlandish salaries for bishops and other Church officials. What the philosophes found most appalling, however, was the control that the Church held over impressionable commoners by instilling in them a fear of eternal damnation. The philosophes may have had mixed feelings about the common people, but they had very strong feelings against the Church. As a result, they provoked the Church by challenging doctrines such as the existence of mira-cles and divine revelation, often disproving specific tenets with simple science. The Church, in turn, hated the philosophes and all they stood for.

LITERACY
Complementing and enabling the socially and politically active atmosphere was the dramatically improving **literacy** rate in France. Beyond just talking about revolutionary ideas, more and more French people, especially in Paris and its surrounds, were reading and writing about them as well. A symbiotic relationship developed as readers anxiously awaited more literature from the philosophes, and in turn the response that the writers received compelled them to write more. The scholarly atmosphere at the time also provided

women of French society—albeit still within traditional roles as salon hostesses—with an opportunity to contribute to the conversation.

MONTESQUIEU

One of the leading political thinkers of the French Enlightenment, the **Baron de Montesquieu** (1689–1755), drew great influence from the works of Locke. Montesquieu's most critical work, *The Spirit of Laws* (1748), tackled and elaborated on many of the ideas that Locke had introduced. He stressed the importance of a separation of powers and was one of the first proponents of the idea of a system of **checks and balances** in government.

Although Montesquieu's work had a great effect on the development of **democracy**, Montesquieu himself believed that no one governmental system better than the others but rather that different forms were better than others in certain situations. An early pioneer in **sociology**, he spent considerable time collecting data from various world cultures, which led him to the rather outlandish conclusion that climate is a major factor in determining the best form of government for a given region. Montesquieu believed that environmental conditions affect behavior and response and thus concluded that governments located in different climates should be adjusted accordingly. Even Montesquieu admitted that this idea worked better in theory than in practice. His legacy therefore lies primarily in his methods, his combination of practicality and Enlightened idealism—ultimately, he was a researcher through and through.

VOLTAIRE

The primary satirist of the Enlightenment, François-Marie Arouet, better known by his pen name **Voltaire** (1694–1778), entered the literary world as a playwright. He quickly became renowned for his wit and satire, as well as the libel claims that often resulted. In and out of prison and other various predicaments for most of his young life, Voltaire spent a period of exile in England during which he was introduced to the works of Locke and Newton. The two thinkers had a profound impact on the young Voltaire, who became wildly prolific in the years that followed, authoring more than sixty plays and novels and countless other letters and poems.

Voltaire was an avowed deist, believing in God but hating organized religion. As a result, he made Christianity—which he called "glorified superstition"—a frequent target of his wit. Voltaire was also an ardent supporter of monarchy and spent a considerable amount of time working toward judicial reform. Later, after bounc-

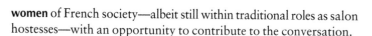

SUMMARY & ANALYSIS

SUMMARY & ANALYSIS

ing around to various countries and working with a number of notable contemporaries, Voltaire wrote the satire **Candide** (1759), which has since earned distinction as one of the most influential literary works in history.

Although Voltaire lacked the practical breadth of some of his contemporaries—he did not dabble in multiple scientific fields—he made up for it with the volume of his work. Using his brilliant, sarcastic wit to analyze everything from philosophy to politics to law, he extolled the virtue of reason over superstition and intolerance and effectively became the voice of the Enlightenment. Moreover, his satirical style enabled him to make incredibly pointed criticisms while generally avoiding serious prosecution by those he attacked. Although detractors complain that Voltaire never offered any solutions to the problems he criticized, he never aspired to do so. Nonetheless, by merely pointing out problems and criticizing different philosophies, he caused considerable change.

DIDEROT

The third major figure of the French Enlightenment was **Denis Diderot** (1713–1784), a writer and philosopher best known for editing and assembling the massive *Encyclopédie*, an attempt to collect virtually all of human knowledge gathered in various fields up to that point. Twenty-eight volumes in length—seventeen text, eleven illustrated—the portion of the *Encyclopédie* edited by Diderot was published one volume at a time from 1751 to 1772. Diderot, assisted by French mathematician **Jean Le Rond d'Alembert** for part of the project, painstakingly collected as much Enlightenment-era knowledge as he possibly could. After Diderot's involvement, an additional seven volumes were completed, but Diderot himself did not edit them.

Beyond just facts, definitions, and explanations, the *Encyclopédie* also included space for philosophes to discuss their thoughts on various topics—although even these opinions were filtered through the lens of scientific breakdown. A veritable who's-who of Enlightenment-era scholars contributed to the collection, including Montesquieu, Voltaire, and Rousseau (*see* Rousseau, *p. 29*). Due to the highly scientific—and thus untraditional—nature of the *Encyclopédie*, it met with a significant amount of scorn. Diderot was widely accused of plagiarism and inaccuracy, and many considered the collection to be an overt attack on the monarchy and the Church.

The *Encyclopédie* was one of the primary vehicles by which the ideas of the Enlightenment spread across the European continent, as it was the first work to collect all of the myriad knowledge and developments that the Enlightenment had fostered. However, the *Encyclopédie* succeeded not because it explicitly attempted to persuade people to subscribe to Enlightenment ideas. Rather, it simply attempted to present all of the accumulated knowledge of the Western world in one place and let readers draw their own conclusions. Not surprisingly, the power establishment in Europe frowned on the idea of people drawing their own conclusions; the Church and monarchy hated the *Encyclopédie*, as it implied that many of their teachings and doctrines were fraudulent. In response to attempted bans, Diderot printed additional copies in secrecy and snuck them out.

Skepticism and Romanticism

Events

1748	Hume publishes *An Enquiry Concerning Human Understanding*
1762	Rousseau publishes *The Social Contract*
1770	Rousseau finishes *Confessions*

Key People

David Hume Scottish thinker and pioneer in skepticism who questioned the human ability to know anything with certainty

Jean-Jacques Rousseau Swiss-French writer and philosopher who espoused democracy in *The Social Contract* and inspired the Romantic movement with *Confessions* and other works

New Movements

As the Enlightenment progressed into the mid-1700s, a noticeable shift occurred away from the empirical, reason-based philosophies of most of the leading French and English thinkers. The new philosophies that developed tended to take one of two major directions. **Romanticism**, a philosophy strongly attributed to **Jean-Jacques Rousseau**, stressed emotion and a return to the natural state of man instead of the confines and constructs of society. **Skepticism**, which gained prominence under Scottish philosopher **David Hume** and was later elevated by German philosopher **Immanuel Kant** *(see Kant, p. 33)*, questioned whether we as human beings are truly able to perceive the world around us with any degree of accuracy. These two movements, along with Church anti-Enlightenment propaganda and increasing unrest as the French Revolution neared, marked a departure from those thoughts that dominated the peak of the Enlightenment.

Hume

David Hume (1711–1776) was a Scottish writer and philosopher who paved the way for the future of the skeptical school of thought. A dogmatic skeptic, he devoted a substantial portion of his work to investigating the limits of human reasoning. Hume began his career in law but soon decided to devote himself to writing and philosophy. His first major work was *A Treatise of Human Nature* (1739), a book that, though now highly regarded, went widely ignored because of its complicated prose. Hume made up for this oversight in ***An Enquiry Concerning Human Understanding*** (1748), in which he rearticulated much of the same material in a more approachable manner.

SUMMARY & ANALYSIS

Hume's studies, which have since become fundamental in modern Western philosophy, focus on reason, perception, and especially morals. Hume questioned whether the senses, and thus perception, could be trusted for a consistent view of the world around us. In considering morality, Hume felt that if a person found a particular action reasonable, then that action was a morally appropriate thing to do. By adding this introspective, individual layer to the issues of perception and morality, Hume stripped the philosophical world of its generalizations.

Indeed, the unrelentingly skeptical Hume believed that everything was subject to some degree of uncertainty—an idea that turned the intellectual world on end. Regardless of how he himself felt about Enlightenment ideas, he kept returning to one thought: because we will never know *anything* beyond a doubt, why bother? Hume also applied his skeptical approach to science and religion, saying that even though neither was capable of fully explaining anything, science was stronger because it could admit that it would never be absolutely correct.

ROUSSEAU

Orphaned in Geneva at an early age, the nomadic and self-taught **Jean-Jacques Rousseau** (1712–1778) drifted about for most of his youth, contributing intellectually however he could. He devised a new system for musical composition (since rejected), submitted articles to Diderot's *Encyclopédie*, and composed essays on various topics. It was one of these essays, *Discourse on the Arts and Sciences* in 1750, which first earned him renown. He followed it up with **Discourse on the Origin of Inequality** (1755), which solidified his reputation as a bold philosopher. This work charted man's progression from a peaceful, noble state in nature to an imbalanced state in society, blaming the advent of various professions and private property for the inequality and moral degradation. Rousseau moved around quite a bit during the next few years but still found time to write two more pivotal works. The novel *Julie, ou la Nouvelle Héloïse* (1761) told the story of a forbidden love, while **Émile** (1762) provided a revolutionary dissertation on the proper way to rear and educate a child.

Émile set the stage for Rousseau's best-known and arguably most influential work, **The Social Contract** (1762). In it, Rousseau describes what he sees as the perfect political system: one in which everyone articulates their wants but ultimately compromises for the betterment of the general public. This **"general will"** would thus contain traces of every citizen's individual will and thus would in some way serve everyone. Rousseau ended his career in solitude, though not before releasing the deeply intimate **Confessions** (1765–1770), an autobiographical piece that chronicled his struggle to stick to his principles in the face of mounting fame and wealth.

As with many of the other philosophes, Rousseau admitted that his idea of the perfect system as outlined in *The Social Contract* was just that—an idea. It wasn't actually in practice anywhere, nor was it likely that it ever would be. In fact, when asked to provide concrete advice to other countries' governments, Rousseau would often give advice that was far more moderate than the suggestions of *The Social Contract*, simply because he knew his ideas would likely not work in practice. In this sense, Rousseau was an idealist, heavily influenced by the "utopian" republics of ancient Greece and Rome, in which each citizen had a vote and a say in the government. In his vision of a perfect world, Rousseau wanted people to be at their most natural state; he hated the idea of "civilized" society and its encroachment on the natural state of man but knew that it was necessary. His frequent denouncements of inequality and the ownership of private property even bore an early suggestion of communism.

ROMANTICISM

Rousseau's emphasis on natural order and the natural state of man, along with his unprecedented autobiographical candor in *Confessions*, ushered in a whole new era of thinking that eventually developed into **Romanticism**. Romanticism stressed a return to life as it can be seen, felt, and experienced and thus encouraged a reliance on emotion, intuition, and instinct as opposed to reason in guiding human behavior. Shakespeare's romantic tragedies were received with a new appreciation during the Romantic era, as were the works of countless other authors and poets that would come to prominence during the next century of Romantic writing.

The innate, approachable philosophies of Romanticism also appealed to the public more so than the pure rationalism and reason of the Enlightenment, which often came across as cold. Although Rousseau certainly was not the only notable Romantic author, he was one of the first, and two of his works resonated greatly with the public. Though certainly not breaking new ground, *La Nouvelle Héloïse* told a story of forbidden love in a relatable manner that struck a chord with readers. Likewise, Rousseau's *Confessions* opened up a whole new world of personal revelation in the genre of autobiography. No previous memoirist had ever discussed his anxiety over the struggle for integrity—nor elucidated his own flaws—so openly. By being so frank and personal, Rousseau not only questioned the developments taking place in the world but also provided a contrast to the cold, sarcastic musings of Voltaire and Hume. People of all classes loved it, and it spawned countless imitators in the decades and centuries that followed.

THE GERMAN ENLIGHTENMENT

EVENTS

1774	Goethe publishes *The Sorrows of Young Werther*
1781	Kant publishes *Critique of Pure Reason*
1785	Kant publishes *Groundwork for the Metaphysics of Morals*
1808	Goethe publishes first part of *Faust*
1832	Goethe publishes second part of *Faust*

KEY PEOPLE

Gottfried Wilhelm Leibniz Mathematician and philosopher; invented many components of calculus; conceived of "spiritual atoms" called monads

Immanuel Kant Skeptic philosopher who formulated idea of transcendental idealism; had enormous influence on later philosophy, especially in Germany

Johann Wolfgang von Goethe Immensely prolific writer whose *The Sorrows of Young Werther* epitomized German *Sturm und Drang* movement; best known for epic verse drama *Faust*

HURDLES TO THE GERMAN ENLIGHTENMENT

The political, social, and cultural layout of **Germany** in the eighteenth century inhibited much of the Enlightenment advancements that took place in France. Germany was divided into a number of smaller states, most of which were ruled by despots who stifled intellectual development. The total number of German newspapers had barely increased at all in the 150 years leading up to the Enlightenment, and the literary language in the country was predominantly Latin, which made the dispersion of other Enlightened works difficult.

Moreover, whereas France had a combination of antsy intellectuals and flighty nobility, as well as a boom in middle-class literacy, Germany did not. Germany lacked the distinct rift between the middle class and the aristocracy, and there was not nearly the popular discontent with religion or the Church that there was in France. As a result, many German intellectuals refuted the French idea of empiricism, refusing to believe that a simplistic set of laws, akin to the laws of physics or astronomy, could dictate the operation of human society. Germany's literary landscape was also quite jumbled: it had no distinct literary style, and different regions pulled from different languages and influences.

THE AUFKLÄRUNG

Nonetheless, after King **Frederick the Great** of Prussia introduced some Enlightenment ideas from other parts of Europe, a small **German**

Enlightenment (often known by its German name, the **Aufklärung**) began, although it went off in an entirely different direction from the English or French movements. The German Enlightenment never subjected religion to the same scrutiny as in other countries; in fact, the Aufklärung retained a somewhat mystical view of the world, with some of Germany's leading writers adhering to the idea of combining reason with religion.

LEIBNIZ

The first major figure in the German Enlightenment was the brilliant **Gottfried Wilhelm Leibniz** (1646–1716), who began his career in law but quickly moved out into other fields. Mathematically, he was Newton's equal, as the gentlemen both "discovered" **calculus** at the same time. Although the two would bicker for some time over proper credit, a few elements of calculus have been attributed exclusively to Leibniz, such as the idea of a function and the integral symbol. Foraying into metaphysics, Leibniz proposed the idea that everything in the universe consisted of **monads**, which he conceived of essentially as "spiritual atoms" that constitute our perception of the world but lack physical dimension. Unlike many figures in the French and English Enlightenment, Leibniz was very religious and in fact saw monads as reflections of a structured, harmonious universe—the work of a perfect God.

Leibniz's deep religious faith and affinity for tradition kept him conservative in his approach to his work, permeated his writings, and paved the way for the mysticism of the rest of the German Enlightenment. Even so, Leibniz laid a foundation that all future Enlightenment scholars would build upon. His monadologial approach to metaphysics may come across as bizarre, but it brought metaphysics into the spotlight and left it ripe for both elaboration and criticism, the latter of which came at the hands of Hume and Kant. Although these two prominent later philosophers disagreed with Leibniz, he gave them something to think about and in that sense enabled their own advances.

KANT

Considered the last major philosopher of the Enlightenment, **Immanuel Kant** (1724–1804) was enormously influential and essentially founded an entire school of thought out of the blue. Living and working in relative isolation in Königsberg, East Prussia, for his entire life, Kant began his career as a tutor and then took a position as professor in a local university. He spent that time, however, studying the works of other philosophers and formulating his own postulates about the world, which he finally released as the **Critique of Pure Reason** (1781).

The *Critique* is a response to the questions that Descartes, Hume, Leibniz, and other contemporaries had posed about perception and reality. Attacking the age-old question of knowledge versus experience, *Critique* proposes that all people are born with an inborn sense of raw experience—a phenomenon that Kant dubbed **transcendental idealism**. Whereas the Enlightenment had been built around the idea that man can *discover* the laws of nature with his mind, Kant countered that it is the mind that *gives* those laws to nature. In so doing, he elevated **skepticism** to unfathomable heights, cemented his place high atop the pantheon of philosophy, and knocked the Enlightenment down a few rungs.

Kant's work with skepticism perfectly sums up the German Enlightenment's mistrust of empiricism. The *Critique* suggests that we all are born with our own ideas and perceptions of the world and, as such, can never know what is "real" and what is "our perception." In other words, reality is in the eyes of the beholder. However, because nothing really exists separate from its existence in the eyes of the observer, then perceptions and observations in the world cannot be trusted. As a result, empirical evidence cannot be trusted either. By thus stating that only a select few universal truths in the world were valid, Kant effectively disagreed with the premise of the entire French Enlightenment.

Kant also tried to define morality, another timeless philosophical question, in **Groundwork for the Metaphysics of Morals** (1785). In this work, he argues that reason must be the basis for moral action and that any action undertaken out of convenience or obedience cannot be considered moral, even if it is the right thing to do. Rather, the morality of an action depends on the *motivation* for the action. Hence, if an individual arrives at the conclusion that a certain action is right and pursues that course of action as a result, then that behavior is moral. These and other ideas of Kant's continued to influence philosophers—especially German philosophers—long after his death. Hegel, Marx, and Nietzsche all borrow significantly from Kant's line of thinking.

GOETHE

Though known less for his philosophy, **Johann Wolfgang von Goethe** (1749–1832) would nevertheless emerge from the Enlightenment regarded as Germany's finest writer. The moody Goethe was prone to alternating between periods of production and remission, but during his times of productivity he churned out two landmarks in German literature. His novel **The Sorrows of Young Werther** (1774), about a young boy who falls for an unattainable girl and eventually kills himself out of despair, had an unimaginable impact on German youth at the time. It is primarily for that work that Goethe is considered the most prominent figure in Germany's *Sturm und Drang* ("storm and stress") movement, a roughly twenty-year period from the 1760s to 1780s in which young German intellectuals, inspired by Rousseau's emphasis on emotion, revolted against optimism and reason and plunged into darker, more anarchic themes.

Goethe released numerous essays, poems, and critiques over the following thirty years, then unveiled the literary masterpiece that would solidify his place in history. The first part of the epic verse drama **Faust** was published in 1808, the second in 1832. The work—a retelling of the German legend of a man who promises his soul to the devil in exchange for knowledge and power (previously told in Christopher Marlowe's 1604 *Dr. Faustus*)—was massively successful. Goethe, however, died the same year that the second part was published.

Goethe was never terribly concerned with the politics of his era, even amid the massive governmental shifts that were taking place in Germany at the time. He was a writer and scholar, plain and simple, and spent the bulk of his career creating an enormous body of literature, translations, and scientific inquiries. *The Sorrows of Young Werther* had such an impact that German youngsters started dressing like Werther and even killing themselves; in subsequent editions, Goethe felt obligated to include a warning discouraging readers from taking their lives. In *Faust*, his monumental foray into satire and social commentary, Goethe continued in his intimate, emotional vein. Between the two parts of *Faust*, Goethe released collections of personal, introverted poetry. Just like Rousseau's works in France, Goethe's works focused on emotions and innate human feelings, signaling the end of the German Enlightenment, which flowed right into the Romantic movement that was burgeoning throughout Europe.

RESULTS OF THE GERMAN ENLIGHTENMENT

Although the pessimism and anarchism of the *Sturm und Drang* movement exposed a one-sidedness to German thought at the time, the movement was brief, and contrasting forces prevailed. A strong nationalistic voice emerged during the German Enlightenment, which did much to unify Germany culturally. Although other factors played in as well, political unity came hand in hand with cultural unity: laws and districts were consolidated, more freedoms were granted to the press, and judicial treatment became more humane. Ultimately, Germany would become a unified nation in 1871.

Other Arenas of the Enlightenment

Events

1717	Handel writes *Water Music*
1758	Quesnay publishes *Tableau Économique*
1764	Beccaria publishes *On Crimes and Punishments*
1769	Watt invents improved steam engine
1776	Smith publishes *Wealth of Nations*
1787	Mozart writes *Don Giovanni*
1791	De Gouges publishes *Declaration of the Rights of Woman and the Female Citizen*

Key People

François Quesnay French economist; advocated less government intervention in the economy in *Tableau Économique*

Adam Smith Scottish economist; espoused hands-off government policies in favor of "invisible hand" of the economy in *Wealth of Nations*

Cesare Beccaria Italian judicial reformer; appealed for fairness in trials and punishments in *On Crimes and Punishments*

James Watt Scottish inventor who vastly improved efficiency of the steam engine, enabling development of factories

Olympe de Gouges French feminist and women's rights activist; wrote landmark *Declaration of the Rights of Woman and the Female Citizen*

Johann Sebastian Bach German organist and composer; wrote a vast body of both sacred and secular music

George Frideric Handel German-English composer; won numerous court commissions and was enormously popular during his life

Wolfgang Amadeus Mozart Austrian composer considered a musical genius and perhaps the greatest composer of all time; created remarkable body of music for orchestra, opera, and voice

Developments in Other Fields

The Enlightenment was not limited to innovations in philosophy, literature, mathematics, and science; in countries throughout Europe, it encompassed new thought and developments in a variety of other academic, artistic, and social fields. Most notable among these achievements were developments in economics, law, industrial technology, women's rights, humanitarianism, and music.

Economics

A common complaint among intellectuals in eighteenth-century Europe was that politics was too closely tied to **economics**. For one, **serfdom**, which kept peasants bound to disadvantageous feudal contracts, was still prevalent, as was the use of tradition and class hierarchy for deciding occupations. Probably the most disadvantageous development was that of **mercantilism**, a much-touted economic system that encouraged governments to closely monitor their import-to-export ratio so as to maintain a favorable balance of trade. Under mercantilism, domineering governments exercised an extraordinary degree of control over their respective economies.

The impetus for change arrived when French economist **François Quesnay** (1694–1774) explained in his *Tableau Économique* (1758) that a natural order of trade, with limited government intervention, would be much more beneficial to both society and the individual. This idea was subsequently elaborated upon and popularized by Scottish economist **Adam Smith** (1723–1790) in his landmark *Wealth of Nations* (1776), which established the nature of economics in three laws: first, that people work more productively when they have self-interest; second, that competition leads to a balanced marketplace; and third, that true supply and demand are a product of free trade.

Smith's advocacy of this **laissez-faire** ("hands-off") economics, as it came to be called, was revolutionary at the time. Simply put, Smith insisted that it is when individuals are most unburdened by trade regulation that they will be most prosperous, because a free system will allow the **"invisible hand"** of the economy to operate. Smith's ideas in *Wealth of Nations* had enormous influence on the Western world and established economics as a science. Numerous modern nations, most notably the United States, implemented Smith's policies and benefited from considerable economic growth.

LAW

The state of European **law** in the eighteenth century was chaotic, as laws were not always written down and court rulings and sentences were often arbitrary and unfair. Aristocratic privilege and religious affiliation provided safeguards against prosecution, while speaking out against either of those institutions was a sure way to *invite* prosecution. During the Enlightenment, however, Italian scholar **Cesare Beccaria** (1738–1794) became a prominent voice in legal reform, questioning in the treatise *On Crimes and Punishments* (1764) how, in such an enlightened age, such atrocious legal unfairness and cruelty could go overlooked. Beccaria demanded that firm legal codes be established based on reason rather than arbitrary decisions and that trials should be open to the public to ensure fairness. In cases of guilt, punishments should be standardized and never involve torture. Beccaria's work was highly influential, and he lived to see a number of European countries adopt his ideas. The French satirist

Voltaire also contributed to the fight for legal reform, albeit using a caustic rather than scholarly voice to point out injustices.

INDUSTRIALIZATION

The **Industrial Revolution** in the Western world in the late 1800s had its roots in Enlightenment-era Europe. Beginning in the mid-1700s, industrialization truly exploded in 1769 when Scottish inventor **James Watt** (1736–1819) substantially improved the **steam engine**, which enabled the development of a primitive **factory system**. Afterward, Europe saw the number of industry-related patents increase tenfold before 1800. The industrial boom had a number of positive effects: it attracted capitalist investors, who in turn precipitated more growth; it created jobs that provided more stability for families; and, as a result, it prompted population growth.

Industrialization was not without its downsides, however. When factories first opened, there was no industrial regulation in place. Factory smokestacks polluted the European landscape so severely that some regions have yet to recover. Poor, willing workers quickly found themselves working grueling eighteen-hour workdays, receiving unfair wages, and facing brutal disciplinary measures. Moreover, without age restrictions on work, it was frequently young children who had to endure such conditions. When workers tried to band together to form early labor unions, they were dissuaded with death threats and other forms of intimidation. Until labor unions finally grew large and well organized enough to command respect, workers had to tolerate the mistreatment.

WOMEN'S RIGHTS

The progressive thought of the Enlightenment also brought calls for increased **women's rights** and equality. **Olympe de Gouges**, a writer and feminist activist in late-eighteenth-century France, solidified the movement with her 1791 *Declaration of the Rights of Woman and the Female Citizen*. An obvious stab at the French Revolution's 1789 *Declaration of the Rights of Man and of the Citizen*, de Gouge's declaration called for equal rights and liberty for women, including more control over marriage.

HUMANITARIANISM

The push for women's rights was emblematic of the changes that were taking place in European society during the Enlightenment. Beyond heightened respect for women, the era also marked the beginning of the end for such atrocious practices as slavery and witch burning. Children, who had previously been treated essentially as miniature adults, began to enjoy more contact and affection with their parents—a shift that owed much to Rousseau's *Émile* and his other Romantic writings. Jews, who had long been ignored or vilified, started to receive a warmer welcome throughout Europe as well.

MUSIC

Given that the Enlightenment had already reinvented pretty much every other field in existence, it's little surprise the era also produced some of Western **music**'s most revered composers. Working during the late **Baroque period** of the early 1700s and the early **Classical period** of the late 1700s, these composers synthesized styles and influences in a wide range of genres of both sacred and secular music.

Johann Sebastian Bach (1685–1750) of Germany quickly built a reputation as a master organist but was also was an enormously prolific composer—a fact that was not entirely appreciated until after his death. His major works include the *Brandenburg Concerto*, his *Mass in B Minor*, the *St. Matthew Passion*, and countless other vocal and instrumental works, both for the Church and for secular purposes.

George Frideric Handel (1685–1759), conversely, found enormous fame as a composer during his life. Born in Germany but working primarily in England, Handel was a celebrated court composer who won numerous commissions and wrote enormously popular operas. Some of his best-known works include the *Messiah*, an oratorio set to biblical text, and the *Water Music*, a suite written for King George I and performed on the river Thames.

The major figure in music at the tail end of the Enlightenment was **Wolfgang Amadeus Mozart** (1756–1791), who ushered in the Classical era. A child prodigy of nearly unfathomable gifts, Mozart was composing music by age six, touring Europe by eight, and writing full-length operas by twelve. As he got older, however, he lacked the business savvy of Handel and, as a result, sometimes had trouble securing work. He worked as an underappreciated court musician for a time before going out on his own, though he remained on the verge of bankruptcy all the while. Mozart died at an early age from an undetermined ailment, though not before finishing an astonishing collection of operas, including *The Marriage of Figaro*, *Don Giovanni*, and *The Magic Flute*. He also wrote more than forty symphonies, significant chamber music, concertos, sonatas, and sacred works and masses, including the famous *Requiem*.

THE LEGACY OF THE ENLIGHTENMENT

EVENTS

1775	American Revolution begins
1776	Paine publishes *Common Sense* Jefferson writes Declaration of Independence
1789	French Revolution begins

KEY PEOPLE

Frederick II "the Great" Prussian monarch from 1740–1786; instituted judicial reforms and created written legal code

Charles III Spanish monarch from 1759–1788; weakened Church influence and implemented other reforms

Catherine II "the Great" Russian empress from 1762–1796; improved education, health care, and women's rights, though continued to crack down on dissent

Benjamin Franklin American thinker, inventor, and diplomat; transmitted many Enlightenment ideas between Europe and America

Thomas Paine English-American political writer; pamphlet *Common Sense* influenced the American Revolution

Thomas Jefferson American author of the Declaration of Independence; drew heavily from Enlightenment political philosophy

ENLIGHTENED ABSOLUTISM

In the later years of the Enlightenment, absolute monarchs in several European countries adopted some of the ideas of Enlightenment political philosophers. However, although some changes and reforms were implemented, most of these rulers did not fundamentally change absolutist rule.

In **Russia**, empress **Catherine the Great**, a subscriber to the ideas of Beccaria and de Gouges, decried torture while greatly improving education, health care, and women's rights, as well as clarifying the rights of the nobility. She also insisted that the Russian Orthodox Church become more tolerant of outsiders. However, she continued to imprison many of her opponents and maintained censorship and serfdom.

In **Austria**, monarchs **Maria-Theresa** and **Joseph II** worked to end mistreatment of peasants by abolishing serfdom and also promoted individual rights, education, and religious tolerance. An admirer of Voltaire, **Frederick the Great**, the king of **Prussia**, supported the arts and education, reformed the justice system, improved agriculture, and created a written legal code. However, although these reforms strengthened and streamlined the Prussian state, the tax burden continued to fall on peasants and commoners.

Spain had a great deal of censorship in place during the early Enlightenment, but when **Charles III** ascended the throne in 1759, he implemented a number of reforms. During his tenure, Charles III weakened the influence of the Church, enabled land ownership for the poor, and vastly improved transportation routes.

ENLIGHTENMENT-ERA FRAUDS

Not all the aftereffects of the Enlightenment were productive. Despite the advances in literacy, thought, and intellectual discussion that accompanied the Enlightenment, middle- and upper-class citizens often mistakenly carried this open-mindedness to an excessive degree. In many cases, this open-mindedness manifested itself in pure gullibility, as supposedly well-educated Europeans fell prey to "intellectual" schemes and frauds based on nothing more than superstition and clever speech.

For instance, during the eighteenth century, people who called themselves **phrenologists** convinced many Europeans that a person's character could be analyzed through the study of the contours of the skull. Likewise, the quack field of **physiognomy** claimed to be able to predict psychological characteristics, such as a predisposition to violence, by analyzing facial features or body structure. Similar medical hoaxes were common throughout the seventeenth and eighteenth centuries, some more dangerous than others, such as the continuing practice of **bloodletting**.

Although many of these misguided Enlightenment scientists believed that their methods could work, many were charlatans who knew exactly what they were doing. The world was wide-eyed and eager for new knowledge and, as of yet, lacked the fact-checking capabilities to separate real discoveries from pure deception.

THE AMERICAN REVOLUTION

Across the Atlantic, the Enlightenment had a profound impact on the English colonies in America and ultimately on the infant nation of the **United States**. The colonial city of Philadelphia emerged as a chic, intellectual hub of American life, strongly influenced by European thought. **Benjamin Franklin** (1706–1790) was the consummate philosophe: a brilliant diplomat, journalist, and scientist who traveled back and forth between Europe and America, acting as a conduit of ideas between them. He played a pivotal role in the **American Revolution**, which began in 1775, and the subsequent establishment of a democratic government under the **Thomas Jefferson**–penned **Declaration of Independence** (1776).

SUMMARY & ANALYSIS

The political writer **Thomas Paine** (1737–1809) also brought Enlightenment ideas to bear on the American Revolution. An Englishman who immigrated to America, Paine was inspired by America and wrote the political pamphlet *Common Sense* (1776), which encouraged the secession of the colonies from England. Later in his life, Paine's religious views and caustic demeanor alienated him from much of the public, and he died in somewhat ill repute.

In many ways, the new United States *was* the Enlightenment, for its leaders could actually implement many of the ideas that European philosophers could only talk idly about. Americans were exposed to, and contributed to, the leading works of science, law, politics, and social order, yet lacked the traditions and conservatism that impeded the European countries from truly changing their ways. Indeed, the Declaration of Independence borrows heavily from Enlightenment themes—even taking passages from Locke and Rousseau—and the **U.S. Constitution** implements almost verbatim Locke and Montesquieu's ideas of separation of power. America was founded as a deist country, giving credit to some manner of natural God yet allowing diverse religious expression, and also continued in the social and industrial veins that were begun in Europe.

THE FRENCH REVOLUTION

Just a decade after the revolution in America, France followed suit, with the **French Revolution,** which began in 1789. Empowered by the political philosophies of the Enlightenment, the French citizenry overthrew the monarchy of Louis XVI and established a representative government that was directly inspired by Enlightenment thought. This harmonious arrangement, however, soon fell prey to internal dissent, and leadership changed hands throughout the years that followed. The instability reached a violent climax with the ascent of **Maximilien Robespierre,** an extremist who plunged the revolution into the so-called **Reign of Terror** of 1793–1794, beheading more than 15,000 suspected enemies and dissenters at the guillotine. (*For more information, see the History SparkNote* The French Revolution.)

Distraught Frenchmen and other Europeans reacted to the tyranny of the Reign of Terror, as well as subsequent oppressive governments in France, by blaming the Enlightenment. These critics claimed that the Enlightenment's attacks on tradition and questioning of norms would always lead inevitably to instability. Moreover, many critics in the nobility saw the violence of the Reign of Terror as

SUMMARY & ANALYSIS

proof positive that the masses, however "enlightened," could never be trusted to govern themselves in an orderly fashion. Indeed, most historians agree that the French Revolution effectively marked the end of the Enlightenment. France itself reacted against the violence of the revolution by reverting to a military dictatorship under **Napoleon** that lasted fifteen years.

LONG-TERM INFLUENCE

Despite the brutalities of the French Revolution and the lingering resentment toward many philosophes, the Enlightenment had an indisputably positive effect on the Western world. Scientific advances laid an indestructible foundation for modern thought, while political and other philosophies questioned and ultimately undermined oppressive, centuries-old traditions in Europe. After several transitional decades of instability in Europe, nearly everyone in Europe—along with an entire population in the United States—walked away from the Enlightenment in a better position. The movement resulted in greater freedom, greater opportunity, and generally more humane treatment for all individuals. Although the world still had a long way to go, and indeed still does, the Enlightenment arguably marked the first time that Western civilization truly started to become civilized.

Study Questions & Essay Topics

Always use specific historical examples to support your arguments.

Study Questions

1. *In what ways did the writings of Comenius and Grotius foreshadow the themes of the later Enlightenment?*

The works of Comenius and Grotius set the stage for Enlightenment thought in a variety of ways. First, the very fact that they were writing in protest of a national event—the Thirty Years' War—was revolutionary, as most European governments up to that point had looked very unfavorably upon individuals who might be seen as undermining their authority. Moreover, the substance of Comenius's and Grotius's arguments contains clear elements that were mirrored in the works of later Enlightenment thinkers. Comenius emphasized the importance of education, claiming that educated citizens would be less likely to go to war. With this suggestion, Comenius made the same argument that the French philosophes would almost a century later—that reason, and the ability to think and analyze a situation, could solve the problems of the world. Both Comenius and Grotius stressed the importance of treating men as individuals, not as commodities—a sentiment that they expressed in different ways. Comenius felt that, physiologically speaking, we are all the same, and it is therefore unnecessary to fight with each other. Grotius wrote that we all have a responsibility to God to use our lives wisely, and thus giving one's life for war is an irresponsible way to die. In short, although they phrased it different ways, both men set forth the same ideas: individual liberty, humane treatment for citizens, and ultimately a change in the way that nations and rulers viewed their citizens.

2.   *Compare and contrast Hobbes's perspective on man
      with Locke's and explain how that perspective affects
      their respective ideal governments.*

Although both hailed from England and both rose to prominence
early in the Enlightenment, Hobbes and Locke took diametrically
opposite approaches in their political philosophies. Hobbes was
steadfast in his belief that all humans are inherently evil or base by
nature. As a result, all people are intrinsically motivated to provide
themselves with as many resources as possible. Because resources in
the world are limited, people thus become selfish and greedy in their
competition for these resources. From this belief emerged Hobbes's
ideal government: one in which a single figure oversees a country
and rules using fear. Hobbes believed that fear was the most effective way to control the citizenry and prevent the disorder that would
result from each individual greedily pursuing his or her wants.

Locke was far more optimistic, stating that all humans were
capable and that they strove for the betterment of the world. His one
caveat was that humans in a society would all have to compromise
on some of their ideals in the interest of forming a government that
best served everyone—however, he believed that humans were reasonable enough to do so. Subsequently, Locke was a proponent of a
representative democracy. Such a system would allow all of these
rational, thinking people in a society to contribute to their gover-
nance, but in such a way that found compromise and kept any one
individual's or group's wants from crowding out the others.

3.   *What factors caused the German Enlightenment to lag
      behind the English and French Enlightenments?*

In the late 1600s and early 1700s, when the Enlightenment was well
under way in Britain and France, Germany was highly fragmented
both politically and culturally. It was technically not a nation at all
but rather a multitude of small sovereign states. Furthermore,
nearly all of these states were ruled by despots who instituted strict
censorship, stifling intellectual development and making the dissemi-
nation of new knowledge difficult. German culture and literature
were likewise disjointed, with different regions drawing on different
influences and no distinct literary style yet in place. Whereas France
and other European countries used vernacular languages for literature, the literary language in Germany was still predominantly

Latin. As a result, Enlightenment ideas from England and France took a long time to spread to Germany.

Moreover, German intellectual culture had a prominent streak of conservatism that was lacking in England and France. Christianity was still a dominant force in Germany, where there was not nearly the level of popular discontent with religion and the Church that there was in other western European nations. Many German intellectuals still incorporated traditional Christian themes into their thought and therefore rejected the Enlightenment's "heretical" focus on pure reason and empiricism. Leibniz, for instance, made a number of great discoveries in mathematics and philosophy, but his religious devotion kept him from straying too far from tradition. As a result, when the German Enlightenment finally did begin in the late 1700s, it proceeded in an entirely different direction from the English and French Enlightenments, embracing reason and rationalism but maintaining strong elements of religion and spirituality at the same time.

QUESTIONS & ESSAYS

SUGGESTED ESSAY TOPICS

1. *Explain Immanuel Kant's philosophy in relation to the search for universal truths. In what ways does he contradict mainstream Enlightenment thought?*

2. *Adam Smith believed that free trade was far superior to mercantilism. In Smith's view, how does mercantilism inhibit economic growth, and how does free trade solve that problem?*

3. *In what ways were the discoveries and innovation of the Scientific Revolution instrumental to the beginning of the Enlightenment?*

4. *Rationalism, skepticism, and romanticism were the three primary philosophical schools of thought during the Enlightenment. Choose one and explain why you feel it's a better approach to life than the others.*

5. *Explain the impact that philosophers from countries other than England, France, and Germany had on the growth of the Enlightenment.*

6. *What evidence is there that the ideas of the Enlightenment continue to be influential in modern times?*

REVIEW & RESOURCES

QUIZ

1. Which of the following was *not* a foundational principle of the Enlightenment?

   A. Relativism
   B. Rationalism
   C. Skepticism
   D. Individualism

2. Which event best represented the shift away from monarchial rule?

   A. The Thirty Years' War
   B. The Glorious Revolution
   C. The Scientific Revolution
   D. The Second Defenestration of Prague

3. Which of the following most influenced the writings of Comenius and Grotius?

   A. The Seven Years' War
   B. The Thirty Years' War
   C. The English Civil War
   D. The American Revolution

4. Grotius is best known for

   A. Advocating a switch away from mercantile systems
   B. Revolutionizing the judicial system
   C. Working in pursuit of women's rights
   D. Establishing rules of engagement for proper warfare

5. Hobbes believed that all humans were inherently

   A. Selfish and evil
   B. Ambitious and motivated
   C. Intelligent and reasonable
   D. Poor and irrational

49

6. Which form of government did Hobbes prefer?

   A.   Absolute monarchy
   B.   Direct democracy
   C.   Representative democracy
   D.   Anarchy

7. 7. Which form of government did Locke prefer?

   A.   Absolute monarchy
   B.   Direct democracy
   C.   Representative democracy
   D.   Anarchy

8. With which philosophical movement was Hume associated?

   A.   Romanticism
   B.   Skepticism
   C.   Mercantilism
   D.   Rationalism

9. King Louis XIV of France died in

   A.   1680
   B.   1695
   C.   1705
   D.   1715

10. Which best describes Voltaire's stance on religion?

   A.   There is no God
   B.   God is everywhere and controls everything
   C.   God set the world in motion but then retreated and
        let it be
   D.   God is dead

11. Montesquieu's political work was based on the writings of

   A.   Newton
   B.   Comenius
   C.   Locke
   D.   Hobbes

12. How many volumes did the *Encyclopédie* ultimately encompass?

   A. Eleven
   B. Seventeen
   C. Thirty-five
   D. Forty-four

13. Which form of government did Rousseau prefer?

   A. Absolute monarchy
   B. Direct democracy
   C. Representative democracy
   D. Anarchy

14. Romanticism changed the direction of the Enlightenment by emphasizing

   A. Skepticism over reason
   B. Empirical evidence over reason
   C. Emotion over reason
   D. Sex over reason

15. Which of the following statements best describes the German Enlightenment?

   A. It embraced the empirical approach of the French Enlightenment
   B. It rejected the empirical approach of the French Enlightenment
   C. It was part of the French Enlightenment
   D. Germany remained wholeheartedly unenlightened

16. How much did religion figure into the German Enlightenment compared to the French Enlightenment?

   A. It had more importance
   B. It had less importance
   C. It had the same importance
   D. All of the above

17. Which choice below has the correct chronological order for the publishing of the listed works?

    A. *Two Treatises of Government, Wealth of Nations, Candide, Encyclopédie*
    B. *Leviathan, On the Law of War and Peace, The Social Contract, Common Sense*
    C. *Leviathan, The Sorrows of Young Werther, Common Sense, Candide*
    D. *Encyclopédie, Candide, The Sorrows of Young Werther, Confessions*

18. The *Sturm und Drang* movement took place in

    A. France
    B. England
    C. Italy
    D. Germany

19. Which work is most closely associated with the *Sturm und Drang* movement?

    A. *Critique of Pure Reason*
    B. *Confessions*
    C. *The Sorrows of Young Werther*
    D. *Candide*

20. Which scientist is credited with devising an inductive method of discovery?

    A. Descartes
    B. Bacon
    C. Newton
    D. Kepler

21. Major strides were made in the field of astronomy thanks primarily to

    A. Kepler and Galileo
    B. Galileo and Newton
    C. Newton and Descartes
    D. Galileo and Bacon

22. Which of the following is *not* a reason for the beginning of the Enlightenment?

    A. Greater exploration led to an appreciation and interest in foreign cultures
    B. The discoveries of the Scientific Revolution changed how people thought
    C. The Thirty Years' War compelled writers to philosophize about the nature of war
    D. The Church encouraged citizens to rely on reason rather than believe in the divine

23. Which of the following sets consists of exclusively English thinkers?

    A. Newton, Hobbes, Locke
    B. Locke, Hume, Kant
    C. Locke, Smith, Kant
    D. Goethe, Paine, Franklin

24. Who was overthrown in the Glorious Revolution?

    A. Louis XIV
    B. Charles I
    C. James II
    D. William and Mary

25. Who ascended to throne during the Glorious Revolution?

    A. Louis XIV
    B. Charles I
    C. James II
    D. William and Mary

26. Identify the correct chronological arrangement of these English events:

    A. *Leviathan* published, Glorious Revolution occurs, *Two Treatises of Government* published, *Wealth of Nations* published

    B. Glorious Revolution occurs, *Leviathan* published, *Two Treatises of Government* published, *Wealth of Nations* published

    C. *Wealth of Nations* published, *Leviathan* published, Glorious Revolution occurs, *Two Treatises of Government* published

    D. Glorious Revolution occurs, *Wealth of Nations* published, *Two Treatises of Government* published, *Leviathan* published

27. In France, philosophes were predominantly

    A. Clergy members
    B. Members of the monarchy
    C. Academics
    D. Rural commoners

28. What best describes the focus of Montesquieu's *The Spirit of Laws*?

    A. Proper government structure, including the division of power

    B. Proper judicial structure, including fair trials and just punishments

    C. Proper economic structure, including a shift from mercantilism to free trade

    D. Metaphysics, including the realization that we cannot trust our senses

29. Montesquieu later developed the theory that

    A. One can identify potential criminals by the shape of
        their face
    B. One can determine the proper government for a given
        region based on its climate
    C. The world consists of tiny, metaphysical building
        blocks called monads
    D. Humans are all born with innate experiences that give
        shape to their world

30. Which of the following did *not* help disperse the
    Enlightenment throughout France?

    A. The *Encyclopédie*
    B. Discussions in salons and coffee shops
    C. The support of the church
    D. Increasing literacy in the country

31. What would govern a civilization in Rousseau's ideal world?

    A. The general will
    B. The Bill of Rights
    C. The Declaration of Rights
    D. The last will and testament

32. Match the author with the correct work:

    A. Locke, *Essay Concerning Human Understanding*
    B. Hume, *Leviathan*
    C. Hobbes, *Common Sense*
    D. Beccaria, *Faust*

33. Which group contains only the works of Rousseau?

    A. *Émile, The Social Contract, Faust, Common Sense*
    B. *Confessions, Wealth of Nations, The Social Contract,
        Common Sense*
    C. *Émile; Julie, ou la Nouvelle Héloïse; The Social
        Contract, Confessions*
    D. *Common Sense; Julie, ou la Nouvelle Héloïse; The
        Social Contract; Confessions*

34. Who was responsible for establishing three laws of motion?

    A. Newton
    B. Leibniz
    C. Newton and Leibniz
    D. Neither

35. Who was responsible for discovering calculus?

    A. Newton
    B. Leibniz
    C. Newton and Leibniz
    D. Neither

36. Who was responsible for combining the schools of algebra and geometry?

    A. Newton
    B. Leibniz
    C. Newton and Leibniz
    D. Neither

37. How did Kant feel about reason?

    A. He embraced it as a logical approach to problem solving
    B. He felt that human perception of the world is relative, so reason is useless
    C. Kant preferred using raw emotion as a guide
    D. Kant liked reason "more than a friend"

38. Which of the following lists contains only German notables?

    A. Kant, Hume, Leibniz, Goethe
    B. Grotius, Paine, Goethe, Kant
    C. Kant, Leibniz, Bach, Goethe
    D. Goethe, Kant, de Gouges, Brunner

39. All of the following were factors that hindered the German Enlightenment *except*

   A. The country was fragmented into a number of oppressively ruled city-states
   B. After the Thirty Years' War, Germans were too busy rebuilding
   C. Religious devotion inhibited Germans from accepting many French philosophies
   D. The written language was predominantly Latin, which was little used elsewhere

40. The main plot device in *Faust* is

   A. A forbidden love
   B. A deal with the devil
   C. An epic quest
   D. A case of mistaken identity

41. What musical period corresponded most closely with the Enlightenment?

   A. Baroque
   B. Romantic
   C. Contemporary
   D. Renaissance

42. Which late Baroque composer was known during his life primarily as an organist?

   A. Bach
   B. Handel
   C. Mozart
   D. Beethoven

43. What man first proposed the idea of replacing mercantilism with a natural order of trade?

   A. Smith
   B. Montesquieu
   C. Quesnay
   D. Greenspan

REVIEW & RESOURCES

44. Smith's pivotal economic work was

   A. *Wealth of Nations*
   B. *Tableau Économique*
   C. *Common Sense*
   D. *The Social Contract*

45. In which field did Beccaria seek reform?

   A. Economics
   B. Law
   C. Religion
   D. Bocce

46. Smith believed all of the following about free trade *except*

   A. People are more productive when they directly affect their income
   B. Competition leads to a balanced marketplace
   C. Free trade guarantees higher profits for a government
   D. Free trade allows supply and demand to drive the economy

47. Which of the following was *not* a factor in starting the Industrial Revolution?

   A. Investors were eager to contribute money to factories
   B. The monarchy subsidized most of the cost of building factories
   C. Cheap labor was readily available and willing
   D. Watt's new steam engine made industry faster and more efficient

48. Which of the following was an immediate downside of the Industrial Revolution?

   A. The economies of industrialized countries collapsed
   B. Industry effectively destroyed religion
   C. Workers were mistreated and forbidden to form unions
   D. Prices of most goods increased

49. All of the following contributed to the end of the Enlightenment *except*

    A. Skepticism
    B. Romanticism
    C. The American Revolution
    D. The French Revolution

50. Paine's *Common Sense* encouraged

    A. People to use reason to solve the world's problems
    B. A switch from mercantilism to free trade
    C. The British colonies in America to declare independence
    D. Safe sex

ANSWER KEY

1. C; 2. B; 3. B; 4. D; 5. A; 6. A; 7. C; 8. B; 9. D; 10. C; 11. C; 12. C; 13. B;
14. C; 15. B; 16. A; 17. D; 18. D; 19. C; 20. B; 21. A; 22. D; 23. A; 24. C;
25. D; 26. A; 27. C; 28. A; 29. B; 30. C; 31. A; 32. A; 33. C; 34. A; 35. C;
36. D; 37. B; 38. C; 39. B; 40. B; 41. B; 42. A; 43. A; 44. C; 45. B; 46. C;
47. B; 48. C; 49. C; 50. C

SUGGESTIONS FOR FURTHER READING

ANCHOR, ROBERT. *The Enlightenment Tradition*. Berkeley: University of California Press, 1967.

ANDERSON, M. S. *Europe in the Eighteenth Century: 1713–1783*. London: Longman Group, 1987.

BERLIN, ISAIAH, ED. *The Age of Enlightenment*. Freeport, New York: Books for Libraries Press, 1956.

DUNN, JOHN M. *The Enlightenment*. San Diego: Lucent Books, 1999.

GOLDMANN, LUCIEN. *The Philosophy of the Enlightenment*. Cambridge, Massachusetts: MIT Press, 1968.

HOF, ULRICH IM. *The Enlightenment*. Oxford, U.K.: Blackwell, 1997.

HYLAND, PAUL. *The Enlightenment*. London: Routledge, 2003.

LIVELY, JACK. *The Enlightenment*. London: Longmans, Green, and Co., 1966.

PENNINGTON, D. H. *Europe in the Seventeenth Century*. London: Longman Group, 1970.

PORTER, ROY. *The Creation of the Modern World*. New York: W. W. Norton, 2000.

PORTER, ROY, AND MIKULÁS TEICH. *The Enlightenment in National Context*. New York: Cambridge University Press, 1981.

REVIEW & RESOURCES

Need More Dates?
SPARKNOTES Can Help!

Try our SparkCharts (only $4.95):

Easy-to-read, laminated chart that fits directly into your notebook or binder.

ISBN: 1411400542 • **African-American History**

ISBN: 1411402634 • **European History**

ISBN: 1586636499 • **US History 1492-1865**

ISBN: 1586636502 • **US History 1865-2004**

ISBN: 1411402693 • **US History Documents**

ISBN: 1586636529 • **US Constitution**

ISBN: 1586636510 • **US Government**

ISBN: 1586637401 • **Western Civilization**

ISBN: 1586636480 • **World History**

ISBN: 1411402707 • **US Map**

ISBN: 1411400682 • **World Map**

ISBN: 1586636677 • **Philosophy**

ISBN: 1586639129 • **Sociology**

Also Available:

ISBN: 1411402890 • **U.S. History AP Power Pack ($14.95)**

ISBN: 1411400933 • **U.S. History Study Cards ($9.95)**

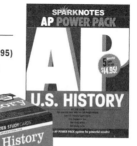

SPARKNOTES